An Alberta Bestiary:

Animals of the Rolling Hills

An Alberta Bestiary

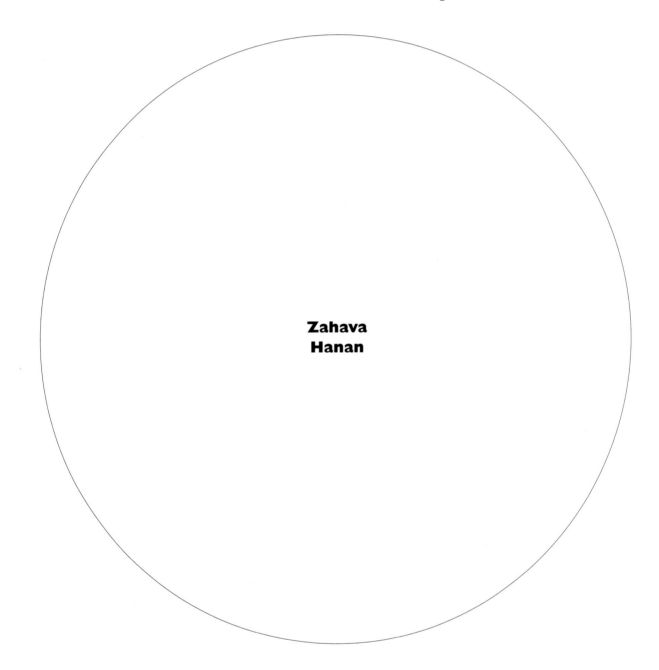

**Zahava
Hanan**

Animals of the Rolling Hills

An Alberta Bestiary
© 2004 Zahava Hanan. All rights reserved.
Published by the University of Calgary Press
2500 University Drive NW
Calgary, Alberta, Canada T2N 1N4
www.uofcpress.com

 Library and Archives of Canada Cataloguing in Publication

Hanan, Zahava
        An Alberta bestiary : animals of the rolling hills / Zahava Hanan.

ISBN 1-55238-158-7 (bound).– ISBN 1-55238-151-X (pbk.)

        1. Hanan, Zahava. 2. Human-animal relationships – Alberta.
3. Animals- – Alberta. 4. Foothills – Alberta. 5. Upland ecology – Alberta. I. Title.

QL221.A5H35 2004   591.97123   C2004-903240-2

With gratitude to the Premier of Alberta, Ralph Klein, and Walter Hildebrandt, who have
facilitated the distribution of this book to all the schools in Alberta.

We acknowledge the financial support of the Government of Canada through the Book
Publishing Industry Development Program (BPIDP).
We acknowledge the support of the Alberta Foundation for the Arts for this published work.

Canadä

Canada Council   Conseil des Arts
for the Arts   du Canada

Printed and bound in Italy by Mondadori Printing, Verona

This book is printed on acid-free paper.

Photography: Zahava Hanan
except page 20, Ardea/Tom, London; page 50, Rosamund Young, Kite's Nest Farm, England;
pages 79,100, Patrick de Marchelier
Drawings: Clarence Tilenius and Abraham Ruben
Editors: Sue Atkinson, Maria Hibbert and Sylvia Reed
Design: Mike Swift
Production: Martin Lee

Every day I am grateful I had my father as a father. I would like to dedicate this book to him, and also two friends who were wise and kind enough to lend me the books which buttressed my Bestiary:

CHARLES DE SALIS
As a boy, Charles travelled around England with his uncle Arthur Collins, the Rector of Staple-with-Barnsole and Shatterling in Kent, in the side-car of his motorbicycle while he photographed ecclesiastical zoology. The resulting book on the symbolism of animals and birds represented in English church architecture inspired me with its gentle lesson that while a parson may preach, animals do the teaching.

NORMAN COHN
A scholar who strayed like me very easily to travel in his mind over the vast Northern sky-lands and white moons. I am grateful to him for delving into the spiritual sagas and primordial barbarous splendour of Siberian heroes and stallions, rescuing them, as he puts it, from their 'long entombment'.

And most important of all, the animals of my ranch in the rolling foothills.

Table of contents

Character is conditioned by place. Aboriginal cultures around the world, especially hunting and gathering cultures, have developed a wisdom about their territories that infuses everyday life and humour, traditional knowledge and what I think of as country grace. *An Alberta Bestiary* by Zahava Hanan is similarly a book that was formed on the land and found its presence on the page through the medium of the author's character. Book and author both embody country grace. As a long-time resident of the Alberta Rocky Mountain eastern slopes along the banks of the Pekisko Creek, Zahava has developed a wisdom about prairie and mountain animals, ranging from buffalo and black bear to horse, gopher, mouse and butterfly. She writes about what she has observed carefully, thoughtfully and with respect. *An Alberta Bestiary* is really a combination of reflections that altogether captures the essence of a life well lived in the eastern lee of the big mountains. It is worth reading slowly and in a spirit of reflection. Even better would be reading *An Alberta Bestiary* out on the land, ideally in the country it describes. And the reader would be well advised to choose a sitting place carefully so as not to crush the blanket of spring croci or disturb the still waiting stones of the Blackfoot tipi rings beside the creek.

M P Robinson, 30 January 2003

Introduction

Brady brought me a gift of a bug house with such excitement, he fell on the top step, splayed out, presenting the present. He told me with concern for the spider within that now the bug was dizzy due to carrying him down the hill to me, but with three sleeps he would be all right. Following this thought, he would bring me a mummy spider to join the dizzy one and if they had six sleeps, they would have babies.

We passed by a seemingly burning bush with fiery autumn colours and he told me flat out 'the caterpillars have been here', and he showed me the delicious bites; I wondered and asked how did he know? He pointed out little holes at the edge of the leaf and in the middle of another leaf, where the caterpillars had had a good time chewing away.

The grass that grew and was not grazed by other creatures was to Brady a rainforest, and I lived the whole summer with him at his grassroots level. Not an imagined innocence, this is innocence caught with a clear eye. Of the bugs all – spiders, bees, helgamites and daddy-long-legs – his favourite was the grasshopper, because it both hops and flies spreading its wings and revealing wondrous colours. Beauty baffles the eye with both this hopper and flier. He has such a sense of self-protection that you do not dare to inch near and he takes off. With his lift-off we share his rattling and clicking, the buzz of the bees, the hum of the flies and the crawling insects, all of nature's music. He found animal paths within the wild bush world and I said, 'Those are our future paths but before you go home, let us go up the hill'. He saw with his child's vision and looking upward, said, 'The future of the animals is up there'.

The bug house gave an extra dimension to me and the Bestiary, so I wanted to thank Brady, and also my husband Ephraim, who was a veterinarian and with whom I had shared the same journey of a primitive need to be ever surrounded by animals.

Animal lore may date back 40,000 years to the earliest inhabitants of the Americas who hunted now extinct species of mammoths, bison and horse.

Hellenistic Alexandria was the cultural metropolis of the world of Late Antiquity and the birthplace of the Bestiary.

The Book of Beasts was the natural history book of the Middle Ages. These ancient bestiaries were formed to give religious and moral lessons that could be learned from animal behaviour.

This Bestiary is written to provide a new grounding for a deeper reverence for animals. Mindful of the invisible tapestry of the creatures of different elements that interplay with each other, sea creatures with land animals, skybirds with water creatures and those that can cross over from one realm to the other.

Many native North Americans still live on the land and rely on animals for food and spiritual resources. They also have great respect for the animals that they believe can take human form. They pray to migrating birds, fish and mammals to ensure they return each year. Maintaining good relationships with animals as non-human persons is vital.

Everything comes from silence.

First the primordial silence, דְּמָמָה דַקָּה the voice of gentle silence before the Holy One appeared.

Then the creation of the Garden of Eden.

My whole landscape of sound this September was full of the hum of summer.

In this hum, the primitive, rhythmic drone of the water flowing in the creek and flies buzzing.

Creation is the language of God. Rhythm is his voice and to sanctify is to sing in unison with him.

Everything created has a voice, everything has a sound; the ocean roars. The earth body and its volcanic thrust has its sound and even the body of water within us. We are eighty per cent water, and within us is the sound of borborygmi. Those who have organic wisdom* can listen to the flow between the body tissues and the organs.

Sound is good.

Silence is good.

*Stuart Korth, osteopath

Bird's voices: the particular kind of song each bird sings has suggested the name we call them.

A human being has many voices, a buried voice, a subtle voice, a voice of wounds, tears uncried and a joyous voice.

Non-human persons have voices too. We are all part of the earth.

Sounds are streaming through this book.

And then, in that acoustical sphere of space, the ancient song, sounds of different realms, dawn chorus at break of day, voices of different creatures, biped, quadruped, walking, crawling, buzzing, flying.

Sounds of the abattoir – killing fields in the urban scape. With humans too the reconciliation of opposites on the earth's surface; joy and sorrow, choral singing resonating up to heaven, chanting East and West, the throat singing of the circumpolar region, the long song singers across the Gobi desert, and alongside that the Wailing Wall of Jerusalem and the howl of the killing fields from Cambodia to the Congo.

The listening field of various animals has ranges other than we do. I pray we can allow for a deeper listening so as to bear witness to sacrificial suffering of non-human persons.

Prologue

One can look down from the sky to a hollow of the earth, home to the indigenous in the foothills of Alberta.

There is in this valley an immense sky resting on an immense earth. The land and house have uninterrupted sight of the rising, arcing and setting of sun and moon, moving through the heavens, all phases visible.

The Chinook arch tells of warmer weather; the joy of a rainbow and the rarity of a white rainbow.

Within the dwelling is solitude and tranquillity, waves spreading out and linking to the beasts, tame and untame.

The breezes outside tell of vibrations and impulses of a spirit wind that move the abysses of mind unconscious, intensely complex threads of memory.

Unconscious, not disconnected from the preparation of centuries, the coordination of many observations and intuitions.

Our little breathings spreading out in gentle streams from us to the creek water and rippling to the Universe.

There is a person there inside the house, with a connectedness between the land and the animals within and without.

The best time for this link is in the lull and silence when all the beings are bedding down.

No words. Silence. The inner oral truth contains the highest truth, a gift from one generation to another.

The ancients had an extraordinary way of keeping truth; that which is written in the soul comes from them.

Night time is the reclamation of dream time with the most intimate passing in of knowledge of the earliest layer of mythology, allowing the human soul to be a wanderer.

At the point of daylight into darkness there is a sharpening of concentration. At that time the imagination is at ease. I can link to the spirit of the First People along with my intellectual inheritance, the Hebrew and Greek myths.

It is stories like these that allow me to be so at ease with the transmutation between man and animal. They venerate the present, forming a link with our forbears and the actual crossing of boundaries of man and animal.

In a dark time the eye begins to see

THEODORE ROETHKE

There is daylight and day-dreaming,
and the night allowing for the unconscious,
and dreaming, nightmares & nightstallions:
God's forgotten language.

When I go out into nature why do I
have immediate intimacy in the immensity?

An Eden Valley Native said to me, 'You are not alone, the ancestors are here. The ancestors of the bear are here too, and a living bear now sees me'.

He has chosen to lean against the foot of a fir tree for his sight line of our homes. I could tell because there I found his bear scat rich with local berries. Bears beat me to the saskatoon berries.

They romp and roll big stones over, having fun turning up big rocks for the delicious fresh protein of insects underneath. Was he having fun amongst the stones on his own? But this may have been a mother and child for small stones were upturned too.

It took me several years to find his trail. The path to it is not people-friendly, for at the base of his hillside there are beaver canals constructed in the marshes. They are clumpy, with uneven mud walls, and hard to manoeuvre.

Compared with most mammals the bear is solitary. I feel at home with his solitariness.

How he watches us (without binoculars!). He knows of watching and thinking and the chords on which to construct a life. The bear is busy with the business of the day. When you see him walk in the landscape, he is in a hurry. He is on his trajectory; he has things to do.

Bears

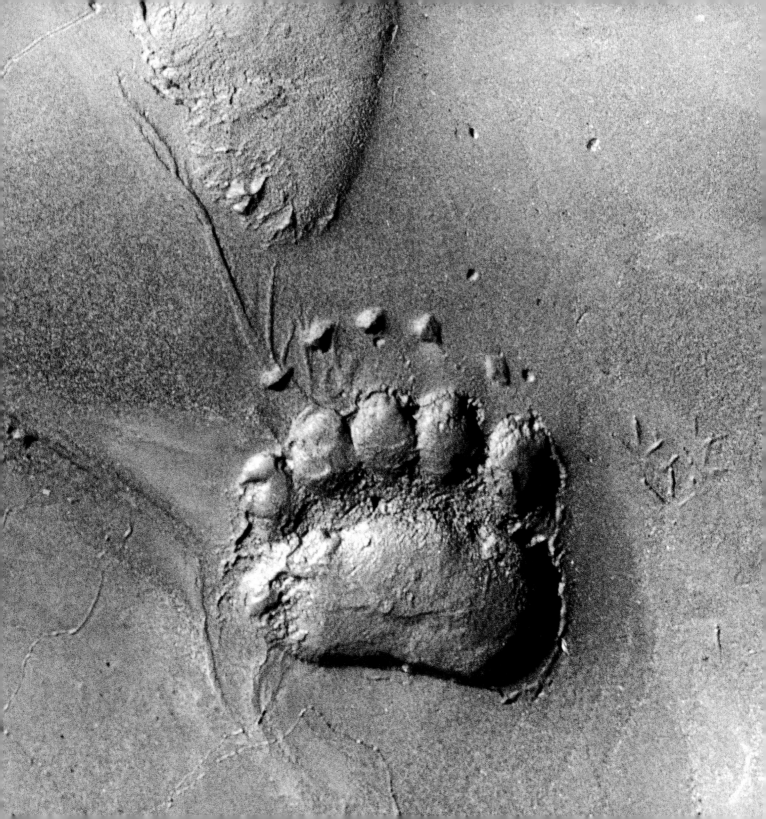

In the beginning he had a pattern. When I was in the Yukon, the Natives still had a pattern with following the caribou in the winter and then with the break of the ice in the spring fishing for salmon. So with the bear, he had some of the same seasonal rhythm, fishing for salmon in the spring.

A bear only goes to a bear den to hibernate when he knows his footprints will be covered by snowfall, so that no one knows he is there. The seasonal pattern of hibernation in the winter; it's a long winter, then the spring and the summer when they love swimming and munching berries and honey. Why are we always bothering them in this short season? Why can we not allow for them? His summer daily routine is just appearing at dawn and dusk, which he does now when it is safest for him.

He knows not only the habits of other animals and mammals, elk and birds; he seems to know more than a man can learn, to sense the coming seasons, and to understand the art of living underground without eating.

Yes, I like the force of his swimming, and he likes climbing and digging and playing and making a bed on which to sleep and love. He too has the dance of the pulse of time on his wrist.

Religions talk of the past and future in the eternity of the moment. The bear has the gift of knowing what is to come from what was, of coherence, sequence and transcendence.

When you look down from a small plane onto my ranch, you see the tame animals in and around the house, then the domesticated animals, and the next surround is the untamed. The deer in the willow bush and bears in the hillside. Five have been sighted. There are tracks in the air for planes, but tracks for us all on the earth.

When I see the old tipi fireplace stones have been rolled over, I know a bear has been seeking fresh ants. When I see molasses-lick for horses tugged over to the other side of the creek, I know she has had a good feed. She not only growls and roars, but makes soft sounds too. The cubs before they emerge from their natal dens, and as they nurse, sound up and down the scale of a sing-song.

The bear is brave and strong, but too, a tender mother.

In an assured and solitary way, the bear seemingly has a secret. The magnitude of a bear going through space is like no other air or atmosphere. The passion is palpable. He is the embodiment of the earth. His walking on the earth is just that: he is the voice of the earth.

The Inuit children came south
to my ranch and were surprised
to see a bear in a black coat.

Weight of a Bear on Water

Everyone remembers the first nest they saw. Close your eyes and imagine all over the world that every creature, bird, insect, mammal, man and even fish sleep, bedding down in their own bedding grounds, whenever their phase of the sun has set and then at the break of day, each moving off in its own rhythm.

As the sun went to sleep and a full August moon arose, I sat at the side of a Canadian glacial lake spell-bound by the reflections on the water, listening to birds about to bed down. When at the still end of day, I heard a big splash and the weight of a bear met the weight of the water and the wave washed and backwashed over him. After he refreshed himself, he strode out alongside the rocks exhaling the biggest breath I ever heard. In that moment, his energy came to me. How wonderful to be part of a circle. This radiating brings resonance to each cell of every living creature. Everything within has to resonate in sympathy with external resonance. A lull as all creatures go to sleep and a change of tempo as we awake; all our breathings interleave.

The bear is earthed. The deer is less grounded and springs between earth and heaven.

Birds and deer are somewhat close in that birds fly and deer leap, and have a kind of anti-gravity. They both spook very easily and take flight in their own way.

I went into the underbrush of a willow wood. I could hear the footfall of the deer. The birds stopped singing, and then the deer heard this and stopped. The underbrush of the old willow wood is where one cannot go on horseback and no one can stand up in it either – you would have to go on all fours. Teleconscious of my presence, the bird is alert and the deer is warned by the bird.

The way a deer springs off and soars tells us his bones must be so different in weight from the bear, and in actual structure. Deer are always fleeing from something. Their flight is wave-like. I feel a deer move through air. There's a spiritedness in the way he moves.

Hearing sound travelling in the breeze, the throat-call of a mother deer, and in her voice is a whole chorus of sounds; each note may have in it suffering or being spooked or a humble plea for sympathy, or forewarning fellow creatures that something is a-foot or a-hoof.

How can one have empathy with a
wandering animal in a wilderness?
But one does.

Linking up through feeling.

The core of the coyote is not only
the beautiful howl at break of day
but the careful observation and concentration
as he leaps for his dinner.

Wolf

A wolf on Ellesmere Island who had not seen one of us before simply had no fright, and came and sniffed and smelt. The wolf was sniffing this new creature with the purity of curiosity.

When I look at the head of a wolf, I see nothing has got in the way of his energy.

Crossover –
Unity, Affinity,
Wild, Tamed

There is a form of contact between a wild animal and a human being. Something in me manages to connect with something in them. The affinity between me and animal life requires treating with caution.

The 'wild animal' has a silence in the deep centre of his being. The magnitude of a bear has the magnitude of a great quiet. Surrounding him is light and energy.

When the bear walks, he is part of the cosmic order: the wild is not irrational.

A bear walking is rhythmical: a city walker may be more animated, but not as rhythmical.

The bear, the horse, the buffalo – will they allow themselves to be subdued?

A buffalo entertained the guests in a hotel lobby in America, but rose up and killed his 'trainer's' father.

If you break a horse in, and do not work with the horse, he will dump the rider one day.

A horse that quickly capitulates, if his mind is injured, will get his own back.

The wild spirit of the horse, the bear and the buffalo cannot be subdued. In the big mammals, down deep, the wild is ever there.

Jim Commodore, a true cowboy, said he and I would not want to raise buffalo, because when you walked into a field their heads would be down. The buffalo, the deer and the elk, when they are farmed, lose their spirit and are inert. One comes upon the same feeling with people in institutions.

I knew the unity with my horse, Farmer, and the true wildness of Joshua, the horse from the hills with no human link.

There are many examples of unity. The unity of horse and man, and elephant and man.

Farmer and I had a unity. Joshua, the wild horse, finds men bring anguish to him so he has to be vigilant to protect himself and for his spirit not to be invaded. Six government men came with a gun loaded with syringes to sedate him. Not only did his spirit reject the lasso, his body even rejected the chemicals. It was so good to see his dignity make a fool of officialdom.

When a beast sees a man in a field,
they always have to flee for their lives. Why?

The beasts have fear and we
share the same emotion.

Is it fear of the focused energy
of a wild animal, or fear of ourselves,
that makes us want to kill them?

I am not fearful of bears: I am ever on the look-out for and wary of wasps. Nothing spooks me as much as wasps. When one is least aware, sitting reading in the grass, relaxing, when wasps are weary and comatose, and suddenly your breath is held, almost ceased: a dying wasp has struck. Then upwells the ultimate, and the urgency of an injection or a life-saving drip at a hospital, which is too far away for comfort.

Something else dawned on me – I put up the first house on this virgin land, with glass windows, of course, and this was a substance that wasps had never met before, and they beat and buzzed and banged against it.

In hot weather not only are the wasps annoyed by the impediment of glass windows, but flies find entry into one's home unimpeded, for they have crawled into the roof shakes, nested and multiplied within their crevices, crawled up and down the wooden walls within and then up and down the inside glass of the windows wanting out. Their wings make their humming music and this goes on all day. Mercifully they like sleeping, too.

Going to sleep. The flies are asleep, fireflies and glow-worms come out. They too are part of bedding-down time.

I find wind is good and cold is good, because it makes the world more fly-proof immediately near me. But I am mindful that they are an essential part of the equilibrium of the earth.

Wasps and Flies

On land, the interplay of bugs, grass and flowers
for creatures; so with the mountain stream,
water bugs and flies for the trout.

Butterfly

In a very dry Alberta summer, when everything was kilned, the only remaining flower was a tall, spindly thistle stem. There I saw a white butterfly visiting this fading plant and because the wind was serious, the two together clinging and swaying in the light-laden air for a long while, clinging and swaying in the wind, dancing to the wind until the butterfly flew near the ground, where it would find it restful.

... Sky flakes down in flurry on flurry...
And now from having ridden out desire
They lie closed over in the wind and cling...

ROBERT FROST *Blue-Butterfly Day*

One time when some news had caused a cowboy friend, Jim, who should be rhythmical, to be rigid and robotic, a butterfly came and landed on the ledge of an open window near us, and just the stillness of the butterfly changed the atmosphere of that room from the contemporary clatter and quietened him.

Jim said once he was riding along and a butterfly rested on his cowboy hat, peering at him under the rim. 'And so I went along for a while, and then I felt embarrassed in case I was taking it in the wrong direction.'

Butterflies teasingly scatter their coloured diamond dust in the flowers' eyes.

HEINE

But there went up a mist from the earth, and watered the whole face of the ground. And the LORD God formed man of the dust of the ground, and breathed into his nostrils the breath of life; and man became a living soul.

GENESIS

In the summer of 2001, I telephoned a friend in Jerusalem, wanting to commiserate in the midst of violence, and her words were 'The butterflies are still flying over the flowers'.

In many lands the butterfly is a symbol of the soul.

Geese

Last spring, on a sloped hillside, where you could peer way down below to a creek, I saw a pair of geese, a couple. One was on the water with the end of his beak and head hanging low and his tail in the water, sitting stock still for a long time. His partner was at the edge of the creek, just gently playing around. I surmised from this that they had just flown in from the south for the summer and were totally tired after a long long flight. I could lie on my tummy on the earth and look down upon them but they could not see me. They were at rest. Had they known of me, it would not have been so restful.

The next day, nearer home, I went for an early-morning visit and they happened to be on the opposite side of the creek and they quacked and quacked and tried tirelessly to quack me out of existence. I knew it was nesting time, but I thought both of us could share the creek, so I stayed for an hour with their quacking going on incessantly.

The next day they had moved away to the other side and they began really informing me to push off. I was a little weary and I thought I would just leave them be in peace and go, respecting their need to create a nest.

As I walked home with my cat, they flew across the creek to start encircling me so very low and close; looking up you could see their beige underbellies. Then they descended and walked up and down, badgering and nudging us out of the way following from their deep need of protecting the nest building.

I had just learned the operative word 'push off' that past year, and they were so clever to know the importance of it so as to protect their place.

Jim and I agreed not to buy any bulls that were brought to the local bull sales, which usually take place in the spring, because these animals have always been overfed on grain; they look huge and impressive, but when they reach the ranch they suddenly lose all this weight which they have put on for auction and become unfit. A rich diet such as oats, barley, beet pulp and alfalfa cubes, which they are given specifically for the sale, is detrimental to their reproductive capacity: their libido, the quality of semen and the sperm reserves are all reduced. You get excess fat on the neck of the scrotum, and it impairs the thermoregulation of the testes. Commercial cattlemen sometimes go for looks and pay a higher premium on fat bulls, but the fact is they have a higher probability of being reproductively deficient. So we went out of our way to find working bulls that had not been given extra feed, and usually we bought them during the coldest weather, so we knew they were good ones and would be able to cope with the worst conditions.

I have often heard men get hung up by a gigantomania – huge bulls with long straight backs and 'not too thin in the pants' (i.e., with fully muscled hips). It is impressive, I suppose, to see a big bull, but some of them have been so raised on the principle that bigger is better that to see them gives me a sense of discomfort. It is the character that draws me. One's character is one's fate; and just as with the rest of us, so with a bull. What is important is first and foremost a bullish character. Apart from this, one looks for a bull with good feet, both to travel over the range after the cow and also to mount that cow.

The University of Alberta suggested that we should not make our bull calves into steers, that is, castrate them. This requires an awareness of the problems of bull management, and of the fact that an effeminate bull – in cowboy parlance 'a sweet-arsed bull' – will be persecuted and ridden by the other more masculine bulls, sometimes literally to death.

Of course, one is seeking bullish character. The odd bull with his effeminacy, or the odd cow that is less than feminine, still keep their masculinity and femininity. The North Pole has not become the South Pole. The bull that is soft and the man who is sensitive are still being so in a male way, just as the cow that is bossy and the woman who is hard are still behaving in a female way. Cowboys always compare cows to women they know.

There is an inverse relationship between dominance and sexual behaviour: the bull that is big on fighting does not always get on with breeding. It is best to mix all the bulls in the herd a few weeks before breeding, so that the social dominance is established.

Since they have been shut away in a bull camp it is odd that, when let loose, instead of thirsting for the ladies they spend days working out seniority, the law of nature ensuring that the progeny are sired by the strongest male.

There is no magic – it is just common sense; Jim Commodore came to work for me precisely because I did not have exotic cattle, because my cattle were average-size animals, and I had no intentions of turning them into beefalo (the result of crossing a cow with a buffalo).

The bull's scrotum is important, an animal having a normal scrotum with a distinct neck has the best development. Large scrotal circumference and good potential sperm production go together. The genetic traits of good testicular size manifest themselves in female progeny, so that selecting the right bull will improve the reproductive potential of the cow. A well-chosen bull will help the cow to have a higher conception rate, earlier pubertal age and calving ease. A good bull is important too because we have such a short season for breeding.

One bull can serve eighteen to twenty-five cows by nature's methods, but up to ten thousand by artificial insemination. Bulls used for this purpose rarely live beyond eight years. At the artificial insemination centres they are kept in runs that might be suitable for dogs and they stand on concrete, because concrete is easier to maintain. But concrete and feet do not mix well. This results in a softening of their feet, and leads to their premature death. The bull's penis is electrically stimulated so that its semen is gathered. Men complain that these bulls are mean bulls, but they do not consider *why* the bulls are so bad-tempered. Would they not also be maddened in such a situation? Bulls' hooves are not provided with the luxury of trainers.

Having obtained the semen for artificial insemination, it is necessary to know which cows are in heat, and therefore in breeding condition. The Gomer bull is used for this purpose. The Gomer bull has been vasectomized, or sexually disabled, and wears a bag of yellow paint around his neck. He mounts the cow in the normal way, and in mounting transfers a splash of the paint to the cow's rear end. He is not able to impregnate the cow, but the cow in heat will be readily identifiable by her yellow behind.

What concerns me is how much we interfere with nature. Some of the implements used to disable bulls from breeding are truly medieval – sometimes in the past, for instance, the bull's organs were wrapped round with cement.

At times men use prods and whips far more than is necessary in moving cattle. Just as humans need to keep a social distance from each other, so with cattle. Cows have their flight field. If the animal is approached carefully and given its space, it will move along its own path and can be eased to where one wants it to be. This takes longer than prodding and whipping, but I have always been amazed at man's ability to turn a blind eye to cruelty. It does not even make economic sense. How often does the free spirit created in the wilderness turn to wild wacko because of desperation and insanity? I have often asked myself that, when I see imbalanced inner stirrings being acted out on the land and its animals.

I feel we must examine our farming practices and consider whether we have the right to defy nature. For instance, it took thousands of years to get the right size of calf for the cow, so as to reach the udder for the first day's suckling of vital colostrum. You cannot make big changes in one or two breedings. Can we not improve our farming methods so that we are able to succeed in the marketplace without all this? The more far-seeing ranchers are beginning to turn their thoughts to this matter.

I have never used artificial insemination. Grenadier, my first bull, came from Scotland, and I went there to choose him. A woman can read an animal as well as a man – it simply requires a tutored eye. In Alberta, buying a bull is generally thought to be cowboy country, but in Scotland there are women who are considered to be good herdsmen, and are thus accepted.

Ronan Nelson at Muckairn, Taynuilt, Oban, whose family owns the oldest Highland herd, mixed this bloodline with the Luing herd to create Grenadier. From his yearling crop he had chosen eight of his best bull offspring for me to see. I chose the two I preferred, but as he had been there at the birth I asked him to make the final choice. With animals, as with humans, the character is present from birth, and even though it may go under for a time, it will always reassert itself. So Grenadier was chosen, took an airplane trip and came to live in Canada.

The hills of Alberta became his kingdom, and he taught me the true meaning of the word 'pushover' as he cleared fences out of his way to make tracks on the earth as he knew he was meant to do, roaming free without boundaries. Sturdy corrals were mere stage sets and no impediment to his travels. He knew his dignified self was not to be boxed into any open-air ghetto.

I was told I was the only one to keep a bull as a pet, for Grenadier would mumble at my front door as he went by roaming in the dusk. He was both aggressive and tender. He put a lot of competitive energy into being top bull on the ranch, but I would often find him in the dawn light lying restfully surrounded by a lot of baby calves.

I would visit him from time to time and just stay with him in the same field and be still. I was always mindful of the way animals spend hours patiently standing and eating rhythmically, and into this field of harmony would come a rush of human hurriers, on horseback or with a truck, because they wanted to move the herd elsewhere or market it.

Kim, my first dog, who sometimes came with me on my herd visits, was in a quandary in the early days, when the animals would approach closer to me and lick my feet – for she had been trained not to bestir the herd. How was she to protect me if she could not bark them away? I could feel confusion in her body, and then she would throw her whole self on my lap as I sat in the field. They, the cows, might lick my feet, but no further were they to go, for her body was a buffer between them and me.

When Grenadier found his way to a neighbour's land, I could tell him to make tracks back home with ease – simply on foot with a stick in my hand which I rarely used. I would say, 'Get on home, Grenadier, there are lots of ladies there', and he would move off waving his head back and forth and emitting much grumbling, but never losing his dignified self.

He insisted on being chief of the bull herd, and there he has remained all his life long. The early days were very busy, and now he is a old man, even though he cannot make out with the ladies or be creative any longer, he still insists on trying to mount them and chase the other bulls away (how like a man!) – to the chagrin of my manager, who feels he is not contributing to the increase of my herd.

You de-horn cows because
they are easier to manage.
This affects their nervous system and
distorts their sense of identity.
I always wince with de-horning.

Snowflake was born on my ranch, an Alberta-born cow of Scottish lineage with a majestic regal crown. So, in a crowd, she could muscle her way through with her head-armour. As the herd's winter feed was laid out in an appropriate circle, nobody inched in on her territory. Seeing that, I thought it was the effect of her great horns or antlers. Looking out from afar on the landscape of the cattle herd at feeding time and seeing her greater horn antler equipment compared to the average Alberta cow (born with smaller horns, and often de-horned), little did I know both the strength, but also the sensitivity of her crown. It dawned on me as our friendship evolved.

The cochlea of my inner ear is the vestigial horn that I carry within me. The cow hears by her horn, it is her inner ear. The horn becomes the ear of the whole metabolism of the cow. When she is chewing the cud, she does not want to be disturbed because she is listening to her inner alchemy.

When she reached cow middle age, she had reared many calves she cared deeply for, so I gave her a foster calf with which she bonded too, even though it lacked the dignity of her own.

But then in the winter period of her life, she wanted to have time to look around and enjoy the world on her own. Then she found amazing shelters, one under a cluster of fir trees protected from the wind, near creek water. With the winter sunset and the coming in of the cold of the long evenings, there in the gloom you could spot her, just after the feeding and the bedding down of the horses in the barn, timing it to eat alone without any grapple, push and shove from the others.

I would heat large buckets of oats so that she could bring warmth into her body when her teeth were not quite good enough to chew old hay and there was not enough grass beneath the snow.

The Cow and the Cat

It was then that I tried carefully to comfort her, and it was then that it came to me that her crown was raw nerve-sensitive and she preferred me rather to stroke her brow.

It was only later that I understood the distinction between the horns and the antlers. The horns grow out of the skin and are rooted and descend into the body like our nails, and the antlers, their polar opposite, are living bone that ascend and ramify from the body like quivering antennae reaching out and up.

So with Willow, my cat, each hair too reaches to outer space. Every hair on her little body has the same properties as the polar bear's where each follicle, like fibre-optics, draws the light and heat from the sun into his black hide. Her hair too needs to be clear, open and unimpeded as a conductor for that which is outside to go within.

The cat has taught me about pure presence; to know about divinity in the moment now. Our preparation for the state of grace may be to brush one's teeth or to sweep the floor; hers is perpetual grooming.

Willow goes out nocturnal hunting and returns before the break of day, which is a very important hour for her. The time between first light and sunrise is the most fragile, precious and secret of all. She feels the purity of the air just before the sun arises.

Upon leaving for a long trip, my suitcases were not in evidence, but she knew and she came to me when I was asleep and put a lot of her dawn clarity into me, purring deeply and pressing her body against mine, in on my breastbone, giving it her full healing, and then left to rest in her own chair. Then in the morning, going away for a long time, which is hard, she feigned sleepiness and just let me go. I felt truly loved. There was so much giving and then so much withdrawing.

The formative principle within
cryptozoic night creatures is a need
to go with rhythm and pattern.
The cat is a night creature who feels
curtailed when there is no
exit to the outside so as to
hunt in the dark.

WILLOW

Her whole body moves with the rhythm of the earth.
Now she's busy full time. Full-moon gazing. Drowsing in the
heat of the sun.

The golden shaft lies still upon the ground
And Willow picks it out
And pauses within it,

Last light shining in the slant beams of the sinking orb,

Sun setting: Willow sitting.
Wherever the sun beams through the trees, there she sits.

Slow wheeling of setting sun, splinter sunbeam rays
And Willow happy and pausing on each splinter
Taking in the presence of last lingering light,

Out to experience the Summer Solstice.

When the light was full and golden,
The path to infinity appeared across the foothills.

Wherever sun beams through the trees, there she sits.

Cat, you are a poem. Up like a flash, eyes emblazoned.
Wherever sun beams through the trees, there you sit.

Mike came from the Glenbow Museum and Lloyd left his herd of
5,000 reindeer on the northern-most coast to come to dinner.
One brought bread and Gao, and the other Norwegian Jarlsberg
cheese. Willow, wanting to be part, brought her first mouse gift
since my return.

Yawns are catching – more fun for me when it is with an animal. Willow yawned and I yawned truly to and fro. My brain yawned – I don't know about hers.

Plants are here to absorb light
Is Willow too?
Walking through tall grass she looks like moving light

Willow, so busy all night out being with the full moon
And all day basking in the sun and rolling on the ground

Willow came in for a little reassurance after a day sun-basking. She has a long tail, her aura goes beyond her tail, way beyond. I, not meaning to, of course, over-stepped with my big shoes on the tip of her tail as she was eating. She spooked, her aura was interfered with – she wanted out of this place and nothing else! It took me a while to tune into the fact that words alone didn't work. Only by my actually loving her, including all of her from head to tail, did she reconnect.

Heat and Willow
Walk and flop
Walk and flop
None of this accustom thy body
Of good school training
In days before Now

Little toes, she has six, does not like paws in snow
Slow to learn to hunt
Not interested in her mother's teaching
Slow developers often are astonishing

Intimacy of the gloaming
And Willow yawns
And her body curling up
And the day is curling up

Mice making their way to the underground
level when the weather cools.

Horns and Antlers

The First people are able to swear on a horn when they are in court; a buffalo horn, a musk ox horn. The Hebrew Nation calls in its people for the High Holidays with a ram's horn.

Antlers first form into a tender blood-filled stage. This is when 'antlering' takes place, when the antler is evolved enough to be filled with blood, but not yet hardened into a solid bone, i.e., to a terrific weapon with pointed tines built for the kill.

The deer, when mature, fight head to head and antler to antler. They go on fighting indefinitely, until the ultimate – one creature falls. A fall means death.

In the plant world the Christmas holly, when young, like the antlers, is soft and tender. When mature, it is very prickly. So the foal and then the ruthlessly grumpy old horse. Are we all soft and tender when young and then the focussed quest for self-preservation creates the prickliness when old?

Farmer

My father had a horse, Farmer, in love with a mare called Melanie – separation from her was awful for him.

I had, after my Father died, a second horse called Farmer. He was a very honest horse in love with Melanie's daughter, Cloudy, in the same intensely loyal way. Both were thoroughbred horses that were racetrack victims.

The horse, wild or not, has a sense of his nobility of movement. When that has been inched in on, destabilized, you can drive him to madness.

Does not everything depend upon the interpretation of the silence around us? The horse teaches you that. In life often the best things happen in a whisper. The horse is a good aid to that listening.

Through him one is seeing wisdom that one has lost in knowledge. May this be a dialogue with myself for soul's sake – one must think about these things.

Is the secret of life to be in touch with your personal rhythm? Rhythm is near the core of everything mysterious and wonderful. I want to put into words that which is quite indescribable. You carry an inner rhythm around with you. The horse is one good easy way of re-meeting rhythm in any digital, rhythm-less society. 'The horse is my drum.'

There is an immediacy of knowing the effect on my Farmer of merely closing your eyes so using fewer muscles. You get yet a different ride when your eyes are straight ahead or eyes are looking upward. It betokens insight. Or just slowing oneself, breathing quietly, you feel him soften. If you hold a bird in your hand, and you hold too tight, you will kill it; if you hold too little, it flies away. How hard to have quiet hands and yet definition in those hands. How to keep hands and reins and horse's mouth quiet with a single hand.

'Focus' in Latin means hearth, home, root, nest. He teaches me focus.

I am totally at home with the Life in Farmer
He is totally at home with the Life in me
To love the Life in us, simply and truly.

Farmer rides me
Something else is riding both of us.
To do it right through the sensory activity may beam you into hierology.

Izaak

The question of silence between living creatures, whether animal or human, is my concern. It is in silence that we learn.

If we have reverence, if we use the eyes of the heart, we will get back to the common language we all once had.

For me that invisible traffic between two creatures is tangible. Izaak and I, he a white horse, I a person, had been together for thirty-seven years. In the deep cold of a January month, his body went flat. When a horse is down and cannot walk, he feels it more than we do. He down and I kneeling beside him, he was not a horse nor I a human, just two creatures sharing pain.

There is clarity in the moment before death and no words can evoke those feelings. No art can tell of the pathos in nature. In the moment with Izaak, I learned of theophany, being both in the pure present and in the eternal – a cross of time – the intersection of time and timelessness. The possibility of different times communicating within a moment.

The Natural Circle

The wind begins in the Pacific, flows over the Rockies and hits my land with nothing having interrupted it.

A quiet surprise on my land for those who delve is a big hidden natural circle. An enclosure encircled by shrubs edging into slightly higher bushes, where the deer are, and then tall dark spruce trees. All gathering to create one circle.

Inside, tall grass is providing a windbreak to the small flowers.

Lying there feeling the wind rise and fall like the ocean wave, I could sense the same silent still point as with one's breathing. The pure still silence is sweetened by the flora.

Waves of air. Time and wind mingle with the blowing top soil, the flowers' fragrance and us.

In the land contours you see waves manifest too.

We link through the long tide

It is a long tide going through us all

The Sound of the Wind

Big Voice of Wind

Wind is God's voice

Throat singing is early Northern
people's answer to the wind

Cat Shooting

Back home on the ranch, despite the sublime setting, the human and irrational thread is ever there.

Mungo was no ordinary man. His shadow was full. There was more than a whisper of cruelty. He was irresistibly fascinated by the gun and the trap, and an expert in both. He had said that his father told him, when you shoot somebody, do it so there is no witness. He was one of the better shots in Alberta, and a devotee of a magazine, 'Guns and Ammo'.

A coyote has a narrow chance of outwitting the trapper and his gun. Mungo once set a trap and inadvertently dropped a dead match nearby and the coyote never went near. But a cat coming out of the door of a house, a gun fixed on her, has not a chance.

Mungo shot my cat when he knew I was safely away for it was the time I was always out riding.

Blackie was this man's dog, but Mungo came back and Blackie would not visit with him. Mungo said, 'He doesn't forgive me for something I did.' There was an inbuilt cruel streak.

My cat's baby was about to follow her mother outside for the first time when her mother was shot and never came back. The baby was given to someone who did not know her history, and she said the kitten would ever retreat from an open door.

Moths — lamps cloistered with moths.
A membrane or caul of moths.

Temple Grundun

Temple Grundun; from her early autism and muteness came her sensitivity to animals' feelings and her skills. This was how she made her living, teaching men to move animals without putting fear and hurt into them.

They asked for her at conferences and they asked for her to design corrals. She was able to access the tough rancher by tough language and economics – that the electric prodding of animals to move them from A to B caused much bruising and financial loss in the end.

A cow and a man; a man walks towards a cow and there is a time when the cow is quiet and there is a threshold of change when the cow takes flight. Temple Grundun could hold back and edge in, timing to move them without stirring them needlessly. If the man walks slowly and does not get too near, the cow will work with him.

She has so much empathy where others have ill-at-easeness.

Noah's Ark

The animals' needs threw a heavy burden on Noah and his family. They had to be fed at the times when they normally ate, day or night. The chameleon presented a special problem: nobody knew what to feed it. Fortunately, Noah let a worm drop from a pomegranate and the chameleon ate it, after which Noah grew worms for the fastidious creature. The phoenix offered to do without food, to save Noah trouble; the patriarch responded by promising that it would never die.

NORMAN COHN *Noah's Flood*

Domestic animals are never as quiet as wild animals. Domestic animals have a hard role between pleasing us and being themselves.

When they are themselves, they have a focus, an energy field; when they are with us, they are polite.

Dogs, they have to go two ways.

A visiting dog from a neighbouring farm, whose work was to keep coyotes away from the sheep, is a good example of two different corresponding instincts. This stray dog that would visit would come in and be polite to the people, the dogs, the horses, and only ferocious when he had to hit out for one of the coyotes.

He could think things out better than most human beings. He had the capacity to figure out what you were and how to work things from there. As hard as he worked the other way, he would try so hard to be good to everyone around.

When he set out to go home, one of the dogs would follow. He would turn on his path in the field and meet his eyes and stare at him for about fifteen minutes. What he was saying to the dog was, seemingly, 'you can be with me when I'm there, but I'm travelling alone'. I suppose I should have sent him back when he crossed the field, but he seemed to need a holiday.

When dogs and cats have people constantly hovering over them, they should be given time and space to be themselves. It is a question of meeting the spirit of the animal.

I like somewhat disobedient animals – then they still have their own spirit.

Domestic: Wild Animals
Dogs who have to be polite

Buckie – Secret Spots

Yesterday I arrived at my secret spot to find a rising of land mists. It began like that, a walk through mizzle (a mixture of mist and drizzle), and then I could go no further because I was actually walking into water. The melting snow running down from the mountain peaks was so abounding that it filled the creek and even flooded my secret spot. Once in winter when it was 40° below I could not go there, and now again I could not reach it. Special places, precious people, are not always accessible or available.

As I back-tracked, this part of the Bible came to me:

For in the wilderness shall waters break out,
And streams in the desert.
And the parched ground shall become a pool,
And the thirsty land springs of water...
And a highway shall be there, and a way,
And it shall be called 'the way of holiness'.

Today I try again, a circumnavigatory route this time. I approach from a different direction by way of an old animal path, curved and winding, which leads to higher ground. Sometimes it takes me under bushes, a little too close to the earth for my height.

Arriving there, I seek a level where it's not flooded. A tree leans over, its upturned roots washed by the flood waters. It may withstand the water flow and recover, or it may float away and end its days.

I find a bit of dry land and make my way to my tree-sit. There's actually a substantial waterfall coming right through a part of the earth's surface. Just standing under this tree trunk, I see three huge waterfalls. The quiet secret spot that was just a little rivulet of water, barely running, now has strong water in three different courses feeding into it. It's become a huge, wide, alive, coursing stream that has flowed down from the mountain tops.

To crawl into a badger hole, up to my knees, inadvertently: to have bitter herbs and sweet herbs; to know the water course – all in a short morning walk ... And Buckie, my dog, is alive with it – the intangible water force has manifested itself in his body and he's bouncing around with it. He's an energy factory, and I've leapt over a stream which would have been impassable before – all from the same creative force.

The Hebrews and Egyptians had a true sense of water; in it they saw the God of Life who springs from the inundation of the mountain snow and dies down with the heat of summer.

The waft of silver willow scent – I am exalted by waves of fragrance, waves of water, flights of birds, flurry, scurry, of gophers leaping. And Buckie and I are somewhere amidst all this movement. I feel elated by the idea that standing on the ground, listening to the rhythms of the earth and the celestial music around us, is a form of prayer. Isn't praying listening to God? The earth rises into land mist, the heavens rain, and in the misty area between heaven and earth we are in the pure numinous present and see many layers of universe reconciled. Happiness in here ... inherent in the moment.

As I walk on I see the forest behind my secret garden all awash. I have never seen such a shift, not since I've known it. Everything is washed out, ready for rebirth. I suppose that's what I am too – about to be reborn. I discover a small tree circle. In their midst, they have twined their roots, appearing as a couple, a triplet, a quintuplet tree family, like five seeds in an apple. A few days later the sound and thrust have gone. The flood water has subsided, leaving an ocean of mud. As the wind blew patterns in the winter snow, so now it has blown similar traces in the mud.

God has totally washed the past and purified it. There will be a lot more regeneration of trees, because the seed harvest of pine cones that the squirrels gathered for winter has been washed into the holes in the earth which they created for their hibernation.

Great hopes for my secret spot after this heavy rain. Later on it will be fascinating to watch nature's effects. Shall I compare myself to this wood?

Tribute to Buckie

*A dog, but he had
no time for anyone who
treated him like a dog*

It is all in the eyes.

What went on when we gazed at each other.

If I tell of Life's light and feeling in them,
nobody will believe me.

Those eyes that shone out in total darkness.

Night eyes, tiger orange beams of light,
as if they came from the stars.
Sky starlight and your starlight.

Your sense of the need for varying behaviour with
each of our fellow creatures, horse, cow, coyote
and then underground, the gopher and badger,
and in the air, birds and butterflies and then me,
ever amazed.

You would stand athwart each horse's head and wait
actively for them to use their scent as you did, for
them to get to know you and to accept all of you.

With the cow you knew not to hurry
and to come at them sideways, not straight on.

With the bull you were more careful and let them get
to know you by sniffing, standing with the barbed
wire fence between you.

With the coyote you were not quite so happy.
You took a bone out to them and came back with the bone
gift ignored, but your own knuckle-bone nibbled.

What followed was a lifetime pursuit of keeping
them out of bounds for they had crossed your
boundaries; you never roamed out but the
air ways were ruffled with coyote howls.

Slanting your neck so silently, listening to movements
of the gophers in their dens and ever waiting at
their entry holes.

With the butterfly or bird you would make an effort
to leap towards them in the air.

Safe in the rapport with yourself and most animals,
your inclusion of me an honour.
You gave me unreserved love.

Whenever I was about to take a trip you took into your jaws
bigger and bigger branches, showing off,
circling around me as if saying
'How can you think of leaving me?
I am so amazing', and I felt so bad.

Then upon my return, grabbing onto a horse's tail,
round and round you go to share with them your
excitement at my return.

When night came, with it came your big dreaming
and chanting. In sleep there was total gravity
in your body, if I tried to lift your front leg,
it was so heavy. I could never attain that state of relaxation.

Once, very near the end, I stretched out on the floor and you threw down your body near me to share with me what you were feeling. I listened closely to the uneven breathing that tells of nearing death.

You received all of me and wished to share your all.

It grieved me to behold you in the last.

Memories of our walks. *As you grew from a puppy you took twigs and sticks, then bigger and bigger lumps of wood and long tree branches in your jaws. Then as you grew older and wearier, they became smaller and smaller again. But the magnitude of your presence never diminished. On our last walk together, a few days before you died, you had little physical energy but came along, pure spirit walking. Your body a vehicle for the mighty spirit within you.*

Your time now drops into eternity.
My thoughts never free from you.
Had I never seen or known you
I would be bereft of all these joys that endeared you to me.

Wanting to backtrack to where you had been and to go back to the memory in feeling of our times together, then and now, I gave up for I began to feel you everywhere I walked.

Your strong spirit strays through these foothills.

Chief John Snow said God created different
countries and different coloured trees and
people.

Red cedar trees and Red Indians are grown in
North America.

The Natives were grown to fit Canada. The
good blend: tipis, fir trees and mountains in
the background with the First People of long
ago on horseback with feather headdresses.

The idea of belonging and the opposite.

Different animals and different flowers fit
different countries.

Land is the history: history is the land

Birds

Birds on still winter trees
Each one picks the tip of a tree
To take in the sun arising
And last warmth of sunset
Heralding the rising Sun
Is that where the Native learned it from?

Brown Black Bird
It would follow me
Flying from tree-top to tree-top
Bush branch
Tree stump
And on the grass.

Oncoming of clouds
Storm in the sky
Many birds lightning-like
Fly past my tipi door
Having just come by the way of the creek alongside
A low fly past
Water level
Now near ground level
Makes sense
With a high and mighty wind.

Through intense sleeting snow
All through the night sky
Thunderings
Infolding lightning flashes its magnetism.

Through many sky lands.
A rushing fills the air.

The Brown Black Bird is fluttering in a pipe
And has slid to the main floor joint where I can see her.
Took a day to cut the pipe
And cover her with a soft cover
And take her to the outer world.

To open our eyes to the dancing rhythms
All the natural forms around us and our ears to the
sound of water
Complete self-abandonment to the immediate event.

Heavenly
Mountain
Snow
Coming
Down
To creek
And earth

Salute to Sun
Natives
Bird

The far fragrance

Eternally pure

Out of high winds' way
Waves of birds fly near creek water
And past my tipi.

Harmony

I live with Keats' pure poetic thought that truth comes through beauty. The apprehension of harmony for me is to be at one with the nature I inhabit.

I work on the reconciliation of opposites. Regaining vitality through the elements.

It took me a long time to admit to the existence of evil, but when it upwells I move back into the perception of harmony; seeking the succession of harmonies is my truth.

The Garden of Eden

I have always wanted to be in the Garden of Eden.

This is my Eden.

Other people have their Eden.

My seeing with the eyes of the First People as
God saw us in Genesis, and saw that it was good.

The Earth obey'd and straight
Op'ning her fertile womb teem'd at a birth
Innumerous living creatures, perfect forms,
Limb'd and fullgrown...

MILTON *Paradise Lost*

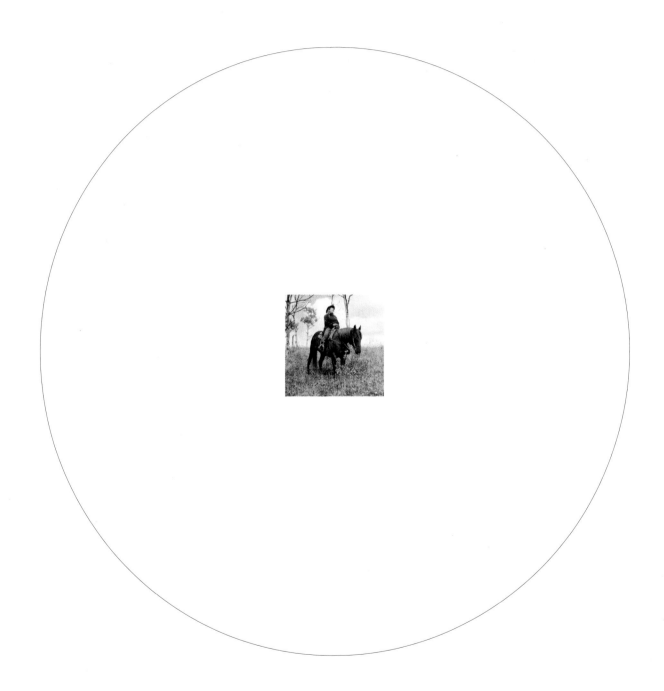

To the memory of Lionel Esher